Gospel Prayers

C. Singer

Gospel
Prayers

1

illustrated by C. Muller-van den Berghe

*I*ntroduction

―――――

When we pray
while looking at Jesus and his actions,
when we pray
while listening to Jesus and his words,
when we pray
while taking in the Good News,
then we begin to work, to take action.
We change our behaviour.
We come out of our shells.
We discover the incredible love
God has for us.
We find the road to happiness.
We create happiness
for the world.
Praying with the gospel
changes our lives!

Jesus says,
"Let the little
children come
to me."
Mark 10:14

Child

I am a child, Lord!
Sometimes I am afraid of making a mistake
and sometimes I am worried
because bad things come from my hands
and my lips.
And yet, I dream
of ten thousand gestures of friendship
and of ten thousand smiles to offer each day!
But how can I do it?

I am a child, Lord!
I am pushed aside,
people tell me that I know nothing,
people tell me to wait and learn.
But how can I grow?

You, Lord, speak words
which increase my courage,
and you walk with me along the road.
You give me the bread of your love,
because you always stay
with those who are small
and not sure of anything.
You are the Lord of children,
the children of today and of all time.

*J*esus says,
"Watch and pray
at all times."
Luke 21:36

Keeping Watch

My mind and my heart are alert
like the eyes of a watchman:
I am waiting, I am looking for you, Lord,
I am one who keeps watch: it is Advent.

I look for you in prayer
and you let me in, Lord,
like a friend who is always there
when I knock at the door.

I look for you in the gospel
and you come to me, Lord,
like a friend who is always there
when I ask for light
to help me travel through the night.

I look for you at Mass, with other Christians.
Through your Word and your Bread,
you come to us, Lord,
like a friend
always ready to offer the best.

We look for you every day
and we see you, Lord,
wherever joy is spread,
wherever lies are rejected,
wherever injustice is stopped.

In order to find you, Lord, we must keep watch,
in our minds and in our hearts!

*B*artimaeus,
the blind beggar,
cried out, "Jesus,
son of David,
have mercy on
me!"
Mark 10:47

Blind

Lord, I close my eyes
in order not to see my parents tired,
my brother alone and lonely,
my friend who is sad
and has no one to console her.

I close my eyes,
I am like a blind person,
and it's by my own choice!
I close myself off in the lair of the night.
I prefer to be alone:
other people bother me.

I close my eyes
in order not to see you, Lord,
waiting to give me the sign
to follow you along the road
where I will grow by serving
like you, Jesus.

Have mercy on me, Lord!
Pull me out of the lair of the night
into which I have buried myself.
Come with your light: then I will open my eyes,
and see you and joyfully follow you
towards my brothers and sisters.

Jesus says, "Heaven and earth will pass away, but my words will not pass away." Mark 13:31

*F*orever

Everything may disappear:
the stars may fall from the sky,
the world may break
into a hundred thousand scattered pieces,
the seasons may disappear
like pencil marks under an eraser,
but we will never come to an end,
because your love, Lord,
is given to us forever,
like a gift of eternity!

Everything may disappear:
mountains may crumble,
the sky may dissolve,
the rainbow may fade away,
the hours and years may be sucked
into the bottom of a giant funnel,
but we will hear forever
the Word you have given, Lord,
like a song of eternity:
"You are my beloved!
All my joy is for you!"

11

A poor widow came and dropped two pennies into the temple collection box.
Mark 12:42

Giving

There are people
who give a lot of money
for the poor.

There are people
who spend a lot of time on their knees,
praying.

There are people
who go to the ends of the earth
to help their brothers and sisters.

As for me, Lord,
I share what I've saved up in my piggy bank,
I pray every day,
I show concern for those who are in pain:
it's nothing unusual, Lord.

But for you, Lord,
what counts
is not that we give a lot,
but that we offer it with all our hearts;
not that we spend a lot of time on our knees,
but that we pray with trust,
that we turn towards others
as though to say,
"See! I don't have much.
But I give it to you,
with all my love!"

*T*he crowds came to John the Baptist and asked him, "What must we do?"

Luke 3:10

*T*o Welcome You

In order to welcome you,
to prepare our earth,
to believe in you,
great Lord,
nothing extraordinary need be done.

I need only have a heart
that is pure and free of deception;
I need only have an attitude
that is kind and free of malice;
I need only put on my lips
a smile and words of joy;
I need only open my hands
in order to give and share;
I need only be attentive and faithful
to your Word;
I need only love,
without keeping track of my kindness.

I need only listen to your call, Lord,
and change my life.

You may come, Lord:
the earth and its peoples
are changing the colours of life
for you.

15

Four Candles

In order to lift
the mantle of darkness
which sometimes covers the world
and even people's hearts, Lord,
and prevents us from seeing you,
I will prepare four candles
and place them at the four corners
of the earth
in order to bring light everywhere:
north, south, east and west,
top and bottom, left and right.
This way, all the people of the earth
will be able to see you
and welcome you.

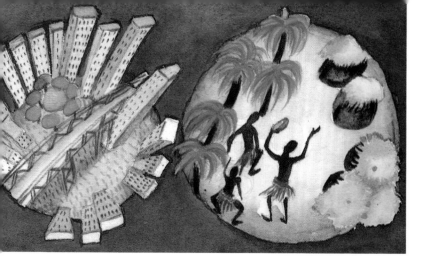

The first candle
will be the light of my smile
bestowed on everyone, every day,
like a gift,
because, Lord, you come
for the joy of all.

The second candle
will be the light of my prayer
turned towards you, every day,
like a long loving look,
because, Lord, you speak
to each of us
in our heart of hearts.

The third candle
will be the light of my
forgiveness
given to all, every day,
like a hand held out
because, Lord, you wash away
all our offences.

The fourth candle
will be the light of my kindness
offered to everyone, every day,
like good bread,
because, Lord, you give your love
to everyone.

In order to show you, Lord,
how I am waiting for you,
I will prepare my four candles,
and I will light them, one by one,
during the four weeks of Advent.

When Christmas comes
in homes and in hearts,
my candles will shine in the night.
They will be my crown of light
prepared for you, Lord,
Prince of Peace.

*E*lizabeth exclaimed, "Blessed are you among women and blessed is the fruit of your womb."
Luke 1:42

Mary

Mary blessed,
Mary chosen,
Mary called,
Mary trusting,
Mary attentive,
Mary faithful,
Mary of the joyous reply!

Mary blessed:
through you, the promised Messiah
is given to us,
through you, the promised blessing,
like a transparent dew,
is spread over the dried-up earth.
Blessed Mary,
lead me to the Saviour.

Mary blissful:
the Son of God,
the fruit of your womb,
Jesus your child
is the happiness delivered by God
to all the children of the earth.
Mary, mother of bliss,
lead me to the Saviour.

Good News

It's Christmas!
Joyous news!

Jesus is born,
a tiny baby, and we see God
looking like babies everywhere.
Jesus is born!
Look: on his lips
we see the smile of God!

Jesus is born, God is here!
Think about it:
God is here,
on the earth where we live,
on the earth where we love.

*"*B*ehold, I bring you good news," said the angel.*
Luke 2:10

Jesus is born, God is here!
He will stay with us forever,
during days and nights.
God is here forever!

Jesus is born:
he will play and laugh and cry;
he will care for the unhappy;
he will stretch out his arms
on the cross,
and we will see God
offering his love
to the whole world;
he will blaze a pathway
through death,

and we will see God
offering his life
to the whole world.

Jesus is born, God is here!
Merry Christmas!

Promise

This night is a night of Promise!
The earth is changing into a big garden,
and in people's hearts
hope appears,
like a flower, a green leaf,
like fruit on an old tree,
like a blade of grass in the middle of winter:
Merry Christmas!

This night is a night of Birth!
A baby is born,
a baby among so many others.
He is like me; he is so little,
but he will become so great
that the whole world will be able
to throw itself into his wide-open arms.
And he has a name which is so beautiful
that I would like to wrap it up and give it to you
to light a smile
on your lips and in your heart:
Merry Christmas!

This night is a night of Joy!
Nobody should be sad,
because God is born on the earth!
So I say to you:
offer joy to everyone
on this night but also tomorrow.
The joy of this night is a gift
for all the days of our lives!
Merry Christmas!

"**Y**ou will find a baby wrapped in swaddling clothes and lying in a manger."
Luke 2:12

Christmas

I sing with the angels,
so that the wondrous news
may reach the vault of the heavens
and the houses of the earth!
Glory to God: he is great and he loves us!
Glory to God: he made himself small
because he loves us!
Glory to God: his love is so great
that he has come to give it to everyone!
Joy to the men and women
and children of the earth.
Christmas!

I run with the shepherds
to admire the small child lying on the straw
in the corner of a poor stable,
and to lay my hand on him and caress him,
saying softly, "You are my Saviour, I love you!"
Christmas!

I stay with Mary and Joseph
to look at the baby wrapped in swaddling clothes,
a newborn bundled and warm.
I stay to look at him for a long time
with a heart so full of joy and music
that it hums its prayer for him.
I stay to kneel before him and say,
"Jesus! Little child like me,
little God-child,
I will stay with you and I follow you,
far along all road."
Christmas!

"We saw his star in the East and we have come to worship him."
Matthew 2:2

*T*he Star

You are the Star, Lord Jesus!
Your gospel
leads the small and the great
towards the happiness God has promised.

You are the Star, Lord Jesus!
Your presence
sheds light on the small and the great,
you kindle in them
the spark of joy
when they are lost in sadness.

You are the Star, Lord Jesus!
Your friendship
warms the small and the great,
you kindle in them
the flame of gentleness
when they are frozen in their malice.

You are the Star, Lord Jesus!
The Star which shines
for all the peoples of the earth!

27

*They fell to
their knees
before him.*
Matthew 2:11

Gifts

Lord of the manger,
I kneel before you
to offer the gold of my love.
You are the Lord whom I love.

Lord of heaven,
I bow before you
to lay down the incense of my adoration.
You are the Lord of the universe.

Lord of the earth
I stand before you
to give you the sweetness of my smile.
You are the Lord of joy.

And you say to me, Lord of the living:
"Your gifts are beautiful
and very precious.
Offer them to your brothers and sisters
of the earth.
Share your smile with them.
Spread your love among them.
Give them your respect.

For whatever you offer
to your brothers and sisters of the earth
you give also to your God."

*T*his is how
Jesus prayed:
"Holy Father, I
have watched over
my disciples…"
John 17:12

Alliance

You make an alliance with me, Lord!
Like a friend, day and night,
you give me your hand.
With you, I am more courageous.
With you, I find it easier to smile;
with you, I find it easier to be joyous;
with you, I find it easier to say "thank you."
You make an alliance with me, Lord,
and making an alliance
means giving each other a hand
to travel along the road together.

You make an alliance with me, Lord!
Like a friend, day and night,
you stay by my side.
With you, I am stronger.
With you, I find it easier to forgive;
with you, I find it easier to chase away the anger
which sometimes grips my heart;
with you, I find it easier
to say no to the desire to do wrong.
You make an alliance with me, Lord,
and making an alliance
means coming together to form a team
because then we are stronger
in the battle against evil.

I am happy, Lord,
to be in alliance with you!

"Unless you are better than the Pharisees, you will not enter the kingdom of heaven."
Matthew 5:20

The Best

You know, Lord, they really should see me:
I am the best!
My mind is like quicksilver;
it runs and roots through every corner
to recall the tiniest detail.
I understand everything sooner than the others,
I know things they don't know;
I am always first, ahead of the others.

You know, Lord, they really should listen to me:
I am the best!
My mouth is always open
like a sounding gong calling for silence.
I know all the answers sooner than the others,
I make everyone laugh,
I speak louder than anyone.
I am the best! I am the... I...

What is that you say, Lord?
"Certainly, you are the best.
But in my eyes,
all the children of the earth
are the best.
For they are all beloved of God.
All are beautiful to look at and to listen to.
People are best because of the treasures
they have in their hearts.
To be the best, you should first
look at and listen to
the marvels and treasures of others."

*J*esus says,
"Every good tree
bears good
fruit."
Matthew 7:17

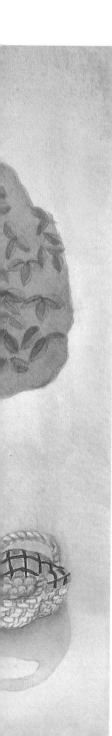

Tree

Look at me, Lord:
with my arms spread out,
my hands open,
and my heart filled with goodness,
I am like a tree!

And I am even bigger
than the tree there in the wood:
because, Lord, I bear fruit in all seasons,
even in winter, when skies are grey
and cold seizes the earth and its people
in an icy grip.

Look at me, Lord, I am like a tree,
and I say to everyone I meet,
Come and eat the fruit of my tree!
Come and share my smile
if sadness has brought you down!
Come and taste my forgiveness
if malice has enveloped you!
Come and pick my friendship
if fear has seized you!
Come and taste my joy
if misfortune has wounded you!
Come to my tree and help yourself!

Look at me, Lord:
just as you asked,
I am a tree which bears good fruit.

Clothes

You know me, Lord!
I don't lie, like Melanie.
I say "good morning" politely,
not like Luke, over there,
who talks like a hooligan.
I don't hurt others, like Cathy.
I don't make fun of people, like Matthew
who sneers at everyone he meets.
I go to Mass,
but Timmy doesn't even know
where the church is.
I don't have tantrums, like David
who turns all red and stamps his feet
if he doesn't get what he wants.
In my case, at least,
it's clear that I'm a Christian.
I'm not like the others over there.

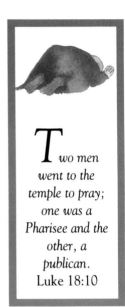

*T*wo men
went to the
temple to pray;
one was a
Pharisee and the
other, a
publican.
Luke 18:10

Today, Lord,
I have put on
my Pharisee garments
which don't have any dirty spots
or holes.

But isn't it true
that beautiful clothes
and impressive words
and perfect gestures
often cover up hearts
which are not clean?
People who think they are the best
do not ask your forgiveness, Lord:
they want only
your congratulations.
They do not ask for
your friendship:
they only want you to give them
a gold medal

for being more perfect
than others.
But you, Lord, prefer
those who are more ordinary,
who do not strut proudly
and dazzle others
with their good deeds.
You prefer those who,
like ordinary people,
feel a bit lost and weak
and who say to you,
as to one they love,
"Lord, we need you."

Lord, you prefer those who,
like ordinary people,
come to pray to you
in garments that are threadbare
from weakness and sin.

*T*he Spirit drove Jesus into the desert where he stayed for forty days.
Mark 1:12

Lent

It is the happy season of Lent!
Christians turn to God
and say: "You are our God!
From you comes all life,
from the beginning and forever!
To you, our Father in heaven,
we give our adoration,
our trust and our praise!"

It is the happy season of Lent!
Christians turn to their brothers and sisters
and say, "You are our neighbours!
To you, our neighbours on the earth,
we will give as much love and joy
as to ourselves!"

For Christians, it is the happy season of Lent:
we need at least forty days each year
to learn with all our heart, all our joy,
all our strength, all our faith
and all our soul
to love God and our neighbour!

For Christians, it is the happy time of Lent:
we need at least forty days each year
to listen to the gospel of Jesus
as to a word, completely new,
coming from the mouth of God,
and to learn to walk
along the same road as the Son of God!

*J*esus says,
"Change your
life and believe
in the
Good News."
Mark 1:15

Ashes

Today, the ashes on my forehead
are the cold remains of a great fire
lit to give light and a soft, golden glow.
    I promise you, Lord: I will be a flame!
    Close to me,
      people will find warmth and courage.
Today, the ashes on my forehead
are the black marks of weeds
which were thrown onto the fire
because they kept the seeds from sprouting.
    I promise you, Lord:
    I will rid myself of the thorns of spite
    and the barbs of jealousy that grow
    in my words and my acts.
Today, the ashes on my forehead
are the unclean spots which cover the spirit
and the heart when I stray from you.
    I promise you, Lord:
    I will become clear as springwater
    by acting like you do in the gospel.
Today, the ashes on my forehead
are what's left of a cracked and arid land
which does not produce any fruit.
    I promise you, Lord:
    I will sow your loving Word
    on my lips and in my heart.
    Then, in my life,
    there will grow heavy sheaves
    of goodness and of forgiveness!

41

*J*esus says,
"Follow me."
Mark 2:14

Change

Wait for me, Lord: I'm coming!
Wait for me, Lord: I'm getting dressed!

I am clothing my eyes with goodness
to look at everyone in friendship.

I am clothing my hands with peace
to forgive without keeping track.

I am clothing my lips with a smile
to offer joy all day long.

I am clothing my body and my heart
with prayer
to turn towards you,
Lord whom I love.

Now I am ready!
It's me! Do you recognize me?
I have put on my best clothing!

*J*esus says,
"You will love
the Lord your
God…
You will love
your neighbour
as yourself."
Mark 12:29-31

P*roof*

What proof can I come up with,
God of my heart,
to show you my love?

I will listen to your Word.
I will keep it like a treasure within me,
and close to you I will feel happy
like a child close to its mother.

What gestures shall I imagine, what marvels,
God of my heart?

I will turn to you to pray
with words born in my soul.
I will kneel before you,
God of the earth and of the universe,
of the dead and the living,
who are all your children.

Today, Jesus, your Son,
tells me what I can do
to show you my love,
God of my heart:
"This is the greatest proof of love for God:
Love those who walk
beside you, along the same road,
give them bread, offer them laughter,
give them happiness every day."

*J*esus says,
"Whoever among
you wants to be
first will be the
servant of all."
Mark 10:43

Serving

With you, Lord Jesus,
it is always the opposite!
The greatest is not the one who commands,
the greatest is not
the one who knows all the answers,
the greatest is not
the one everybody recognizes,
the greatest is not
the one who has gold and silver,
the greatest is not the one who is strong
and who shouts and makes people afraid.

With you, Lord Jesus,
we become great
in heart and in love
when we are ready to serve.

47

Serving is difficult.
That is why I approach you
to learn how to serve:
forgiveness instead of vengeance,
a smile instead of anger,
friendship instead of spite,
joy instead of sullenness.

Serving is difficult.
That is why I look at you,
Servant Jesus, who gave everything,
to serve happiness
to the entire world.

G*o!*

I would like so much to be
a friend of God's.
I would like so much to love
and admire and listen to
and stand before God
in full sunshine!

I would like so much for God's Word to be
the joyous news announced
at every hour of every day
in every place in the world!

*J*esus says,
"Go, sell what
you have."
Mark 10:21

I would like so much to
create happiness
like an enormous cake
and to share it with everyone,
so that everyone could have
a taste!

I would like so much to
distance myself
from lies that are dark
like the night,

and say only words of truth,
clear as a morning
high in the mountains!

You look at me with love,
Lord Jesus,
and you say,
"You really want it? Then go!
Do not wait any longer.
I will help you.
It is time you started off."

"If you love me, you will keep my commandments."
John 14:15

With You

You, Lord,
are astonishing!

With you,
we learn that life should be shared,
like bread given out to all,
like nourishment.
We are hungry for love.

With you,
we learn that God
entered the land of suffering,
where heart and body are torn,
in order to stay with those
who cannot go on any longer
under the weight of the cross,
and to soothe them with your outstretched arms.
We are hungry for hope.

With you,
we learn that joy
always comes in the early hours,
when everything appears to be over,
and that God himself sees to it
that the stones of death
are rolled aside and broken forever.
We are hungry for eternity.

With you, Lord Jesus,
there is passion for life.

*H*e is risen!
Mark 16:6

*E*aster

The Lord Jesus has gone
from the darkness of the tomb
to the glittering light:
it is Easter!

The Lord Jesus has gone
from death to life:
it is Easter!

Death barred his way
but Jesus repelled death.
Through him the way to life has been opened:
it is Easter!

53

With you, Risen Lord,
I take the path of life:
I leave behind the death of spiteful words
and I take on kindness;
I abandon the dark lies
for the light of truthful words;
I forsake blows and mockery
and I hold out my hand to ask forgiveness;
I push sin far away from my hands and my heart;
I believe in you, Lord of life,
Conqueror of death!

You see, Lord, with you
        I am already on the path of Life!
            With you, Risen Lord,
                I go forward on the road
                    to Easter!

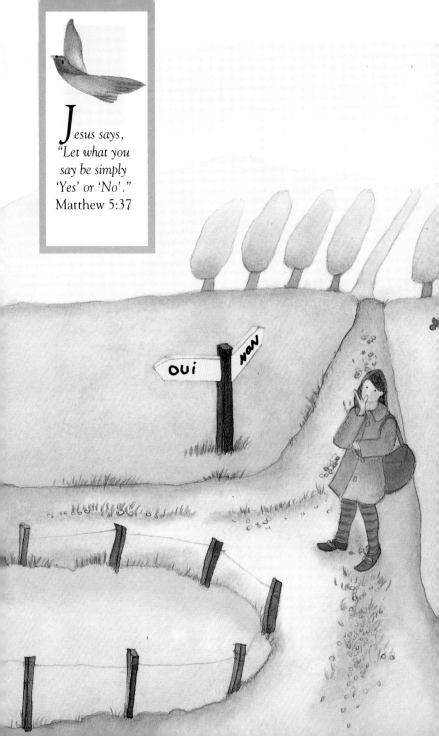

*J*esus says,
"Let what you
say be simply
'Yes' or 'No'."
Matthew 5:37

I Can

I cannot dance
on sunbeams,
I cannot fly
on the wings of the wind,
but if I want to,
I can say, "Yes,
I forgive you,
you who made me cry!"

I cannot soar
above the mountains,
I cannot sleep
on pillows of clouds,
but if I want to,
I can say, "No,
lies will not come
from my lips!"

I cannot float
among the stars,
I cannot travel
on the Milky Way,
but I can say, "Yes!"
I can say, "No!"

Thank you, Lord, for the joy
of being free and able to choose!

55

*J*esus said to
Pilate, "My
kingship is not of
this world."
John 18:36

King

Christ, Son of God,
King born in a stable,
King who loves the humble,
King who looks for friends,
King of the joyous news!

Christ, Son of God,
King of the poor,
King of the sick,
King of sinners,
King of forgiveness,
King who cures!

King who embraces children,
King of a single law: "Love one another."

King servant,
King on his knees to wash the feet of his friends,
King broken and given out like bread to eat,
King crowned with thorns,
King with arms nailed,
King come from the tomb,
King repelling death,
King of Life!

Jesus Christ,
our Lord and King!

*T*he word of
God came to
John, the son of
Zechariah, in the
wilderness.
Luke 3:2

Today

Today, Lord,
a regular day of joy and pain,
an ordinary day of work and play,
today, a day like any other day,
you speak to me:

"How can the world hear
the gentle music of my great love
if you do not play the melody
through your words and your deeds?
You are the singer of my Word!

"How can the world hear
my loving Word
which consoles the desperate
who have fallen to the bottom
of a dark ravine?
You are my spokesperson!"

Today, like every day
you speak to me, Lord:

"Prepare the way for God,
who comes to sow
the seeds of happiness
in the rocky soil of the world!"

Jesus says, "Be perfect as your heavenly Father is perfect." Matthew 5:48

Saints

They choose to be poor,
for they believe that there exist treasures
more precious than silver and gold.

They learn to cry,
for they believe that every tear
will be transformed into joy.

They choose to be gentle,
for they believe that this will give them strength
to sow beauty on the earth.

They choose to hunger for justice,
for they believe that in the eyes of God
all human beings are equal.

They choose to be merciful,
for they believe that to relieve misery
is to act like God.

They accept persecution,
for they believe that to give one's life
fosters community.

They accept to be insulted because of Jesus,
for they believe that to follow Jesus
means to go through mockery and the cross.

These are the saints, Lord!
This is the beautiful name given to all
who choose to travel your road to happiness.
Today, I join them on the road!

You and I

You and I,
if we talked to each other
about our laughter and our tears,
if we took each others' hands
to run and play,
if we looked at each other
with care and tenderness,
it would be good —
like sitting around a big table:
there would be room for everyone,
nobody would be left out,
we would no longer be afraid,

we would no longer be alone.
Life would be as beautiful
as a rainbow!

You and I,
if we stopped beside the Lord,
if we turned to him
with our hearts and our faces
in order to pray and admire him,
we would then have the courage
to live like God's children
and like brothers and sisters
of all the people of the earth!

Then there would be a bridge
of light
between the Lord and us,
beautiful as a pure
and weightless song
flying straight to the heart
of the sun!

Text: Charles Singer
Artwork: Chantal Muller-van den Berghe
Design: Studio Bernadette Bayle
Layout: Robert Vienneau
Translation and adaptation: Zonia Keywan

Originally published in France as *Prières d' Evangile*.
English text prepared under the direction of Novalis,
Saint Paul University, Ottawa, Canada.

Published in association with Editions du Signe,
by McCrimmon Publishing Co. Ltd.,
10-12 High Street, Great Wakering, Essex SS3 0EQ

ISBN 0 85597 511 3

McCRIMMONS

10-12 High Street
Great Wakering
Essex SS3 0EQ
Tel: (0702) 218956
Fax: (0702) 216082